DATE DUE

Holiday ★ Histories

Election Day

Mir Tamim Ansary

Heinemann Library
Chicago, Illinois

© 2002 Reed Educational & Professional Publishing
Published by Heinemann Library,
an imprint of Reed Educational & Professional Publishing,
Chicago, Illinois

Customer Service 888-454-2279
Visit our website at www.heinemannlibrary.com

Designed by Depke Design
Printed and bound at Lake Book Manufacturing

06 05 04 03 02
10 9 8 7 6 5 4 3 2

Library of Congress Cataloging-in-Publication Data
Ansary, Mir Tamim.
  Election day / Mir Tamim Ansary.
    p. cm. -- (Holiday histories)
Includes bibliographical references and index.
  ISBN 1-58810-221-1
  1. Elections--United States--History--Juvenile literature. 2.
Election Day--History--Juvenile literature. [1. Election Day. 2.
Elections--History. 3. Holidays.] I. Title.
  JK1978 .A198 2001
  324.973--dc21
                                    2001000071

Acknowledgments
The author and publishers are grateful to the following for permission to reproduce
copyright material:
Cover photograph: Corbis
p. 4 The Photo Works/Photo Edit; p. 5 Dwayne Newton/Photo Edit; pp. 6, 18, 20, 23, 27, 29 Corbis;
pp. 7, 17 SuperStock; pp. 8, 9, 12 North Wind Pictures; p. 10 Reuters, Jim Bourg/Archive Photos;
p. 11 Paul Conklin/Photo Edit; pp. 13L, 13R, 14, 16 The Granger Collection; p. 15 Private
Collection/The Bridgeman Art Library; p. 19 Bill Foley/Bruce Coleman, Inc.; p. 21 Robert
Brenner/Photo Edit; p. 24 AP/Wide World Photos; pp. 25, 26 David Young-Wolff/Photo Edit; p. 28
Robert Brenner/Photo Edit.

Every effort has been made to contact copyright holders of any material reproduced in this book.
Any omissions will be rectified in subsequent printings if notice is given to the publisher.

Some words are shown in bold, **like this.** You can find
out what they mean by looking in the glossary.

Contents

An Exciting Tuesday

It is early November. Most children are in school, and most grown-ups have gone to work. Yet there is excitement in the air.

What makes this Tuesday special?
It is **Election** Day. Most adults who
are at least eighteen years old get to
vote. And tomorrow, we may have
new leaders.

★

Election Day in the Past

Seventy-five years ago, **elections** were quieter. There was no television. It took longer to find out who had won. But Election Day was a day for **voters,** just as it is today.

Elections have been taking place since 1789.
That is the year our **government** was
formed. Our country was brand new then.

Creating a Government

In those days, most countries had kings. People did not choose their kings. Kings were all from the same family. But the American **colonists** decided to try a different **system.**

They set up a democracy. In a democracy, the people choose the leaders. They can also replace leaders they do not like.

Benjamin Franklin (left) and Alexander Hamilton (right) helped set up our democracy.

Our Elected Leaders

In our democracy, we **elect** a president and vice president every four years. The president is the leader of the country. The vice president helps and takes over if the president dies.

We also elect the people who make our laws. And we elect people to run our states, our cities, and even our schools.

Our First Elections

We had our first **election** in 1789. George Washington was elected president. He had led the war against the British. His vice president was John Adams.

John Adams

Thomas Jefferson

In 1796, John Adams was elected as our second president. His vice president was Thomas Jefferson. Then, Jefferson became our third president in the 1800 election.

★

Election Day Is Born

Even from the start, **elections** were held in November. But at first, people in different places could **vote** on different days. In some places, the voting could go on for days.

But in 1845, a new law was passed. It said everyone must vote on the same day. Election Day would be the first Tuesday after the first Monday in November.

★

Who Can Vote?

At first, only some Americans could **vote.**
Women, for example, could not vote.
Neither could **slaves.** Sometimes, poor
people were kept out of **elections,** too.

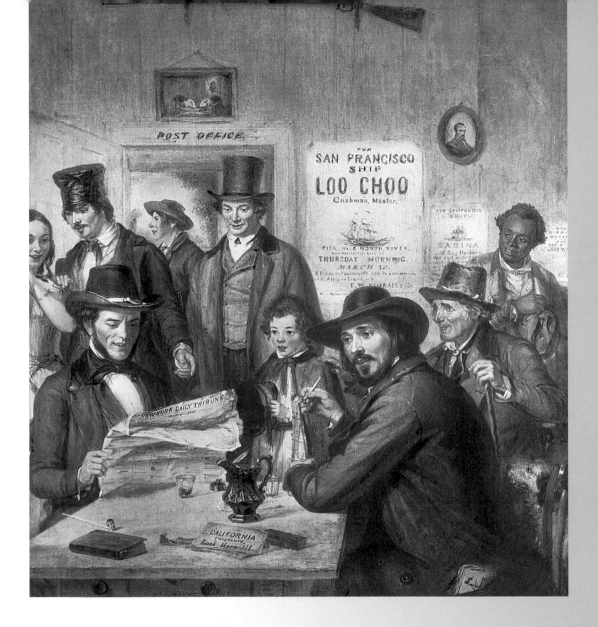

All that has changed. Today, almost any
citizen who is at least eighteen years old
can vote. But people must sign up as voters
before Election Day.

★

Who Can Be President?

Only certain people may be president. They must be over 35 years old and born in the United States. And no one can be president more than twice.

Except for these points, anyone may **run** for this **office.** The president can be a man or a woman. He or she can be of any **race** or religion.

*Jesse Jackson ran for president in the 1984 and 1988 **elections.***

★

What Are Campaigns?

People who want to get **elected** to an **office** are known as **candidates.** Many candidates may try for the same office.

The candidates try to get people to
vote for them. They give speeches, run
advertisements, and shake hands. This
is called a campaign.

Radio and Television

Long ago, people often did not hear or see the **candidates.** They only read about them in the newspapers. Then, radio and television were invented.

Before television, people got their news from radios like this one.

Now, candidates have advertisements on radio. They also appear on television almost every day. Radio and television play an important part in today's **elections.**

Where Do We Vote?

On **Election** Day, you may see flags outside certain buildings such as schools, churches, and libraries. These are polls, which are places were people can **vote.**

People do their voting in a **booth.** No one can watch them. They do not have to tell anyone how they voted. They can vote as they please.

What Is a Ballot?

Each **voter** gets a card called a **ballot**. Listed on this card are all the **candidates**. Voters make a mark or punch a hole next to their choices.

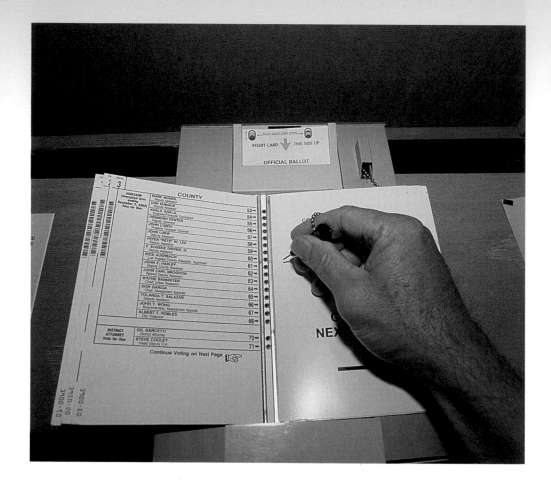

In most places, voting ends at 8 P.M. After that, the ballots are gathered and counted. The winners are usually announced that night or the next day.

Voters Rule

Voters have the most important job in our **government.** They choose the people who will be our leaders. Voters have the real power.

Next **Election** Day, notice who is campaigning for which **office.** Ask yourself who you would vote for. Someday, after all, you will be running the country—as a voter.

Important Dates

Election Day

1776	The Declaration of Independence is signed
1787	The rules of our democracy become law
1789	George Washington is **elected** president
1845	The date for Election Day is fixed by law
1870	Former **slaves** get the right to **vote**
1920	Women get the right to vote
1944	Franklin Delano Roosevelt is elected president for the fourth time. He is president for over twelve years.
1951	Presidents are limited to eight years in **office**
1971	Eighteen-year-olds get the right to vote

Glossary

ballot card voters use to show their choices

booth small closet-like space

candidate person who runs for a job or position

citizen member of a country

colonists people who live on land controlled by
   another country

election choosing of people for jobs, positions, or honors; to
   choose someone by voting is to elect

government all the people who govern a country, state,
   city, or town

office job in the government

race group of people with the same ancestors

run to enter a race or contest

slaves people who are owned by and work for other people

system way something is done

vote to make one's choice; people who vote are called voters

More Books to Read

Oates-Johnson, Mary. *The President: America's Leader.*
   Austin, Tex.: Raintree Steck-Vaughn, 1996.

Scher, Linda. *The Vote: Making Your Voice Heard.*
   Austin, Tex.: Raintree Steck-Vaughn, 1996.

Steins, Richard. *Our Elections.* Brookfield, Conn.:
   Millbrook Press, 1998.

Index